THE HYMN

OF THE

ROBE OF GLORY

BY

G. R. S. MEAD

1908

BIBLIOGRAPHY.

Wright (W.), Apocryphal Acts of the Apostles (London, 1871), ii. 238-245.

Nöldecke (T.), Rev. of Wright, Zeitschrift der deutschen morgenländischen Gesellschaft (1871), pp. 670-679.

Macke (K.), "Syrische Lieder gnostischen Ursprungs. Eine Studie über die apocryphen syrischen Thomasacten," Theologische Quartalschrift (Tübingen, 1874), pp. 24-70.

Lipsius (R. A.), Die apocryphen Apostelgeschichten u. Apostellegenden (Brunswick, 1883, 1884), i. pp. 292-300; ii. pt. ii. p. 422.

Bevan (A. A.), The Hymn of the Soul--Texts and Studies (Cambridge, 1897), vol. v., no. 3.

Hilgenfeld (A.), Rev. of Bevan, Berliner philologische Wochenschrift (Berlin, 1898), xviii., no. 13, pp. 389-395.

Burkitt (F. C.), The Hymn of Bardaisan. Printed at the Press of the Guild of Handicraft, Essex House (London, 1899); 300 copies only printed.

Bonnet (M.), Actes de Saint Thomas, Apôtre. Le Poème de l' Âme. Version grecque remaniée par Nicétas de Thessalonique. Extrait des Analecta Bollandiana (Bruxelles, 1901), tome xx. pp. 159-164.

Bonnet (M.), Acta Apostolorum Apocrypha (edd. Lipsius et Bonnet), vol. ii., pt. ii (Leipzig, 1903), pp. xxii., 219 ff.

Hoffman (G.), "Zwei Hymnen der Thomasakten," Zeitschrift für die neutestamentliche Wissenschaft (Giessen, 1903), vol. iv. pp. 273-294.

Preuschen (E.), Zwei gnostische Hymnen (Giessen, 1904).

Burkitt (F. C.), Rev. of Preuschen, Theologisch Tijdschrift (Amsterdam), May, 1905, pp. 270-282.

F. = Mead (G. R. S.), Fragments of a Faith Forgotten (2nd. ed., London, 1906).

H. = Mead (G. R. S.), Thrice Greatest Hermes (London, 1906).

PREAMBLE

The original title of this beautiful Gnostic Poem has been lost, and it is now generally referred to as The Hymn of the Soul. Preuschen, however, calls it The Song of Deliverance (Das Lied von der Erlösung); while in my Fragments (1900) I ventured to name it The Hymn of the Robe of Glory. I here, also, prefer to retain this title, as it seems the more appropriate.

The original text of the Poem is in Old Syriac, in lines of twelve syllables with a cæsura, and so in couplets, for the most part of six syllables. A text of a Greek version has recently been discovered by Bonnet at Rome (C. Vallicellanus B. 35) and published in his text of The Acts of Thomas (1903). It is partly literal, partly paraphrastic, with occasional doublets and omissions of whole lines. In addition there is a summary in Greek by a certain Nicetas, Archibishop of Thessalonica, who flourished prior to the XIth century (the date of the MS. in which his abridgment is found), but who is otherwise unknown. This seems to be based on another Greek version.

The copy of the original Syriac text is found in a single MS. only (Brit. Mus. Add. 14645), which contains a collection of Lives of Saints, and bears the precise date 936 A.D. Our Poem is found in the text of the Syriac translation from the Greek of The Acts of Judas Thomas the Apostle; it has, however, evidently nothing to do with the original Greek text of these Acts, and its style and contents are quite foreign to the rest of the matter. It is manifestly an independent document incorporated by the Syrian redactor, who introduces it in the usual naïve fashion of such compilations.

Judas Thomas on his travels in India is cast into prison. There he offers up a prayer. On its conclusion we read:

"And when he had prayed and sat down, Judas began to chant this hymn: The Hymn of Judas Thomas the Apostle in the Country of the Indians."

After the Poem comes the subscription:

"The Hymn of Judas Thomas the Apostle, which he spake in prison, is ended."

This literary phenomenon is precisely similar to that presented by The Hymn of Jesus (Vol. V.), to the introduction of which the reader is referred for a brief consideration of the nature of the Gnostic Acts.

Our Hymn is indubitably Gnostic; but of what school or tradition? Learned opinion is preponderatingly in favour of attributing it to the Syrian Gnostic Bardais~n (Gk. Bard' sán' s-- 154-122 A.D.), or, less precisely, to some Bardesanist poet. (For Bardesanes, see F. pp. 392-414).

This is borne out by the text of the Poem itself, in which the mention of the Parthians (38a) as the ruling race is decidedly in favour of its having been written prior to the overthrow of the Parthian dynasty in 224 A.D.

There are also other indications pointing to Bardais~n as the poet; not only are some of the leading doctrines peculiarly those of this distinguished teacher, as has been pointed out by Bevan and Preuschen, but also, as I have ventured to suggest, there is a certain personal note in the Poem.

Bardais~n's parents were rich and noble; and their young son not only received the best education in manners and learning procurable, but he was brought up at the court of Edessa with the crown prince, who afterwards succeeded to the throne as one of the Abgars. Not only so, but Bardais~ n subsequently converted his friend and patron to Gnostic Christianity, and induced him to make it the state-religion; so that our Gnostic must have the credit indirectly of establishing the first Christian State.

The description of the trade-route from Parthia to Egypt and of the adventures of the hero in Egypt, moreover, has led me to ask whether a real piece of personal biography may not have been woven into the Poem. May there not be in it a lost page from the occult life of Bardais~n himself?

Filled with longing to penetrate the mysteries of the Gnosis, he joins a caravan to Egypt, and arrives at Alexandria. There he meets with a fellow-countryman on the same quest as himself, who gives him some useful hints about the many corrupt and charlatanesque schools of pseudo-gnosis that thrived in that centre of intellectual curiosity and religious enthusiasm. He, however, in spite of these warnings, seems to have fallen into the hands of the unscrupulous, and so, for a time, forgets his true spiritual quest, in the by-ways, perchance, of lower psychism and magic. Only after this bitter experience does he obtain the instruction he longs for, by initiation into the spiritual Gnosis of the inner circles of, it may have been, the Valentinian tradition.

Of course this speculation is put forward with all hesitation; but it is neither impossible, nor improbable.

In any case, it is the least important element, and need not detain us except as being a possible source of the local colouring matter. The Hymn itself is a truly poetic inspiration, and deals with far higher mysteries and experiences. But before we can venture to suggest an interpretation, the reader must be made acquainted with the Poem itself in a version based on a minute comparison of all the existing translations.

THE HYMN.

When, a quite little child, I was dwelling

In the House of my Father's Kingdom,

And in the wealth and the glories

Of my Up-bringers I was delighting,

From the East, our Home, my Parents

Forth-sent me with journey-provision.

Indeed from the wealth of our Treasure,

They bound up for me a load.

Large was it, yet was it so light

That all alone I could bear it.

Gold from the Land of Gê l~ n,

Silver from Ganz~ k the Great,

Chalcedonies of India,

Iris-hued [Opals?] from Kã sh~ n.

They girt me with Adamant [also]

That hath power to cut even iron.

My Glorious Robe they took off me

Which in their love they had wrought me,

And my Purple Mantle [also]

Which was woven to match with my stature.

And with me They [then] made a compact;

In my heart wrote it, not to forget it:

"If thou goest down into Egypt,

And thence thou bring'st the one Pearl--

"[The Pearl] that lies in the Sea,

Hard by the loud-breathing Serpent,--

"[Then] shalt Thou put on thy Robe

And thy Mantle that goeth upon it,

 "And with thy Brother, Our Second,

Shalt thou be Heir in our Kingdom."

I left the East and went down

With two Couriers [with me];

For the way was hard and dangerous,

For I was young to tread it.

I traversed the borders of Maish~ n,

The mart of the Eastern merchants,

And I reached the Land of B~ bel,

And entered the walls of Sarbā g.

Down further I went into Egypt;

And from me parted my escorts.

Straightway I went to the Serpent;

Near to his lodging I settled,

To take away my Pearl

While he should sleep and should slumber.

Lone was I there, yea, all lonely;

To my fellow-lodgers a stranger.

However I saw there a noble,

From out of the Dawn-land my kinsman,

A young man fair and well favoured,

Son of Grandees; he came and he joined me.

I made him my chosen companion,

A comrade, for sharing my wares with.

He warned me against the Egyptians,

'Gainst mixing with the unclean ones.

For I had clothed me as they were,

That they might not guess I had come

From afar to take off the Pearl,

And so rouse the Serpent against me.

But from some occasion or other

They learned I was not of their country.

With their wiles they made my acquaintance;

Yea, they gave me their victuals to eat.

I forgot that I was a King's son,

And became a slave to their king.

I forgot all concerning the Pearl

For which my Parents had sent me;

And from the weight of their victuals

I sank down into a deep sleep.

All this that now was befalling,

My Parents perceived and were anxious.

It was then proclaimed in our Kingdom,

That all should speed to our Gate--

Kings and Chieftains of Parthia,

And of the East all the Princes.

And this is the counsel they came to:

I should not be left down in Egypt.

And for me they wrote out a Letter;

And to it each Noble his Name set:

"From Us--King of Kings, thy Father,

And thy Mother, Queen of the Dawn-land,

"And from Our Second, thy Brother--

To thee, Son, down in Egypt, Our Greeting!

"Up an arise from thy sleep,

Give ear to the words of Our Letter!

"Remember that thou art a King's son;

See whom thou hast served in thy slavedom.

Bethink thyself of the Pearl

For which thou didst journey to Egypt.

"Remember thy Glorious Robe,

Thy Splendid Mantle remember,

"To put on and wear as adornment,

When thy Name may be read in the Book of the Heroes,

"And with Our Successor, thy Brother,

Thou mayest be Heir in Our Kingdom."

My Letter was [surely] a Letter

The King had sealed up with His Right Hand,

'Gainst the Children of B~ bel, the wicked,

The tyrannical Daimons of Sarbā g.

It flew in the form of the Eagle,

Of all the winged tribes the king-bird;

It flew and alighted beside me,

And turned into speech altogether.

At its voice and the sound of its winging,

I waked and arose from my deep sleep.

Unto me I took it and kissed it;

I loosed its seal and I read it.

E'en as it stood in my heart writ,

The words of my Letter were written.

I remembered that I was a King's son,

And my rank did long for its nature.

I bethought me again of the Pearl,

For which I was sent down to Egypt.

And I began [then] to charm him,

The terrible loud-breathing Serpent.

I lulled him to sleep and to slumber,

Chanting o'er him the Name of my Father,

The Name of our Second, [my Brother],

And [Name] of my Mother, the East-Queen.

And [thereon] I snatched up the Pearl,

And turned to the House of my Father.

Their filthy and unclean garments

I stripped off and left in their country.

To the way that I came I betook me,

To the Light of our Home, to the Dawn-land.

On the road I found [there] before me,

My Letter that had aroused me--

As with its voice it had roused me,

So now with its light it did lead me--

On fabric of silk, in letter of red [?],

With shining appearance before me [?],

Encouraging me with its guidance,

With its love it was drawing me onward.

I went forth; through Sarbā g I passed;

I left B~ bel-land on my left hand;

And I reached unto Maish~n the Great,

The meeting-place of the merchants,

That lieth hard by the Sea-shore.

My Glorious Robe that I'd stripped off,

And my Mantle with which it was covered,

Down from the Heights of Hyrc~nia,

Thither my Parents did send me,

By the hands of their Treasure-dispensers

Who trustworthy were with it trusted.

Without my recalling its fashion,--

In the House of my Father my childhood had left it,--

At once, as soon as I saw it,

The Glory looked like my own self.

I saw it in all of me,

And saw me all in [all of] it,--

That we were twain in distinction,

And yet again one in one likeness.

I saw, too, the Treasurers also,

Who unto me had down-brought it,

Were twain [and yet] of one likeness;

For one Sign of the King was upon them--

Who through them restored me the Glory,

The Pledge of my Kingship [?].

The Glorious Robe all-bespangled

With sparkling splendour of colours:

With Gold and also with Beryls,

Chalcedonies, iris-hued [Opals?],

With Sards of varying colours.

To match its grandeur [?], moreover, it had been completed:

With adamantine jewels

All of its seams were off-fastened.

[Moreover] the King of Kings' Image

Was depicted entirely all o'er it;

And as with Sapphires above

Was it wrought in a motley of colour.

I saw that moreover all o'er it

The motions of Gnosis abounding;

I saw it further was making

Ready as though for to speak.

I heard the sound of its Music

Which it whispered as it descended [?]:

"Behold him the active in deeds!

For whom I was reared with my Father;

"I too have felt in myself

How that with his works waxed my stature."

And [now] with its Kingly motions

Was it pouring itself out towards me,

And made haste in the hands of its Givers,

That I might [take and] receive it.

And me, too, my love urged forward

To run for to meet it, to take it.

And I stretched myself forth to receive it;

With its beauty of colour I decked me,

And my Mantle of sparkling colours

I wrapped entirely all o'er me.

I clothed me therewith, and ascended

To the Gate of Greeting and Homage.

I bowed my head and did homage

To the Glory of Him who had sent it,

Whose commands I [now] had accomplished,

And who had, too, done what He'd promised.

[And there] at the Gate of His House-sons

I mingled myself with His Princes;

For He had received me with gladness,

And I was with Him in His Kingdom;

To whom the whole of His Servants

With sweet-sounding voices sing praises.

* * * * *

He had promised that with him to the Court

Of the King of Kings I should speed,

And taking with me my Pearl

Should with him be seen by our King.

COMMENTS.

THE PEARL.

Both Hoffmann and Preuschen are of opinion that the Poem is a free elaboration of the chief element in the very briefly recorded Parable of the Pearl which the first Evangelist alone has preserved (Matt. xiii. 45, 46):

"Again the Kingdom [or Kingship] of the Heavens is like unto a merchantman seeking fine pearls; and when he found a pearl of great price, he went and sold all he had and bought it."

This seems hardly sufficient in itself to account for the genesis of our Poem. Certainly for the Gnostics, if the Pearl meant the Kingdom of Heaven in the sense of the Gnosis, it also meant something more definite and intimate, and in all probability the tradition of the mystic meaning went back to pre-Christian days.

Thus the pre-Christian Hellenistic initiate who was the first commentator of the Naassene Document, quotes a mystery-saying of the Phrygians--? from the Mysteries of the Great Mother--as follows:

"If ye have eaten dead things and made living ones, what will ye make if ye eat living things?"

On this the Jewish commentator, who was in high probability a contemporary of Philo of Alexandria--let us say about the first quarter of the first century--writes:

"And by 'living things' they mean logoi and minds and men--the 'pearls' of the Inexpressible Man cast into the plasm below."

Those logoi, or "words" or "reasons"--that is spiritual minds or true "men"--are the "angels" who perpetually behold the Face of the Father, that is live in the Divine Presence. The Inexpressible Man is the

Transcendant Logos, and the logoi are His sons. In brief the Pearl is the "Higher Self."

Later on, in the same Document, the Christian Gnostic writer, who further comments on the interpretation of the Jewish exegete, adds:

"That is what He saith:

"'Cast not the holy thing to the dogs nor the pearls to the swine.'"

And on this finally the Church Father Hippolytus remarks:

"For they say that the work of swine is the intercourse of man with woman." (H. i. 175).

It is to be noted that in the Chaldæan Oracles (ii. 26 ff.) "dogs" are a technical term for a certain class of "daimones"; so also "swine" may for the Gnostics have designated another class.

In any case we get the equation, pearl=logos; that is, the "light-spark," the ray of the Logos, the Christ-nature in man. And so also in The Acts of John we read the following, in a hymn of praise put into the mouth of John, at the sacred feast prior to his departure from the body. It is addressed to the Christ, and the sentence that concerns us runs:

"We glorify the Resurrection shown unto us through Thee; we glorify Thy Seed, Word (Logos), Grace, Faith, Salt, True Pearl ineffable." (F. p. 440).

It is thus evident that the Pearl is in some way the mystery hidden in man, and, indeed, buried in the body. For "Egypt" is the body.

EGYPT.

Thus in the same invaluable Naassene Document, the Jewish commentator, quoting from some still more ancient commentary, writes:

"This is what is written:

"'I have said, Ye are Gods and all Sons of the Highest'—if ye hasten to flee from Egypt and get you beyond the Red Sea into the Desert."

And to this he himself adds in further explanation:

"That is, from the Intercourse Below to the Jerusalem Above who is the Mother of the Living."

And then he resumes his quotation from presumably some old Jewish Gnostic commentary:

"But if ye turn back into Egypt—(that is, to the Intercourse Below)—'Ye shall die like men.'"

And on this he again remarks:

"For all the Generation (Genesis) Below is subject to Death, but the [Birth] begotten Above is superior to Death."

And, speaking of the Great Ocean of Genesis, he continues:

"This is the Great Jordan, which, flowing downwards and preventing the Sons of Israel from going forth out of Egypt, or the Intercourse Below, was turned back by Jesus [LXX. for Joshua] and made to flow upwards."

After "Egypt" the Church Father Hippolytus interjects the gloss:

"For Egypt is the body, according to them." (H. i. 163, 164).

All of this Gnostic allegorizing is, in high probability, to be assigned to pre-Christian Chassid and allied (e.g. Therapeut) circles, similar to those which developed the ethical teaching of The Testaments of the Twelve Patriarchs, which Prof. Charles has, in his just published text and translation, so brilliantly conjectured to have been written about 109--106 B.C. This ethic, he contends, influenced very strongly the writers of the New Testament documents, and anticipated some of the most characteristic Sayings of Jesus.

How the symbolism of Egypt, the Red Sea, the Desert, and the Promised Land, was developed by these Mystics may be seen from what Hippolytus (Ref. vi. 16) summarizes of the system of the Peratæ or Transcendalists, who were contemporaries of the Naassenes.

The Gnostic treatise that the Church Father had before him, was treating of the Great Water or Ocean of Genesis that moistens the soul and plunges it into the Region of Death, according to the word of Heraclitus:

"For to souls water becomes death."

The Peratic writer continues:

"This Death overtakes the Egyptians in the Red Sea together with their chariots [sci. vehicles]. Now all who are ignorant [sci. are without the Gnosis] are Egyptians."

Hippolytus then summarizes as follows:

"And this, they say, is the Going-forth out of Egypt--out of the body. For they consider that the body is a little Egypt, and that they cross over [or transcend--hence their name Peratæ] the Red Sea (that is, the Water of Destruction, which is Kronos [that is, Time]), and reach a state beyond the Red Sea (that is, Generation), and enter the Desert (that is, reach a state free from Generation), where there are all together the Gods of Destruction and the God of Salvation."

And the Peratic writers adds:

"Now the Gods of Destruction are the Stars [that is, the Fate-spheres] which bring upon sentient beings the necessity of changeable Generation [Genesis, the Br~hmanical and Buddhist Sams~ra].

"These Moses called the Serpents of the Desert who bite and destroy those who imagine they have crossed the Red Sea.

"To the Sons of Israel, therefore, who were being bitten in the Desert, Moses revealed the True Serpent [sci. of Wisdom], the Perfect One; and they who believed on Him, were not bitten in the Desert (that is, by the Powers).

"No one, therefore, is thus able to save and deliver those who come forth from the Land of Egypt (that is, from the body and from the world), save only the Perfect Serpent, Him who is full of [all] fulnesses.

"He who centres his hopes upon Him, is not destroyed by the Serpents of the Desert (that is, by the Gods of Generation)."

It is thus evident that for these mystical allegorists Egypt stood for both the body and also the hylic or gross-material realms, and that the use goes back along the Naassene-Ophite trace to pre-Christian Jewish Gnostic circles. It is, therefore, unnecessary to bring forward later passages from Clement of Alexandria and Origen in confirmation of the use.

THE PARABLE OF THE PRODIGAL.

That our Poem is simply an elaboration or embellishment (Ausschmückung--Preuschen, p. 66) of the briefly-recorded Parable of the Pearl, as has been supposed, is a very insufficient hypothesis to account for its genesis. Even if we were so inelastic as to imagine that it must necessarily have its point of departure in canonical scripture, we might more appropriately surmise that it is rather an elaboration of the beautiful Parable of the Prodigal, which is recorded by the third Evangelist alone (Lk. xv. 11-32).

That, however, it is something far other than a mere embellishment even of this beautiful Parable, must be evident to the most casual reader. There is originality in it, and its resemblances may, with far greater probability, be referred to knowledge of the inner facts that both Parable and Poem set forth, rather than to any slavish following of the canonical text. Still it is well to remark the resemblances:

The Father and the two Sons, of whom the younger goes forth; the dividing up of the substance (oὐs...a) or living (b...oj); the far country; the joining himself to a citizen of that country--the reverse in the Poem; the eating the food of swine--the symbol of generation; the calling to remembrance of the Father's household; the return; the running of the Father to meet him, as he speeds to meet the Father, and the kissing of him; the putting on of the robe.

It is, however, evident that the whole matter is treated from another standpoint; it is far more intimate and reveals a full insight into the spiritual mysteries.

In the Parable there is no mention of the Divine Mother, the Queen of the East; and this is in keeping with later Rabbinical exclusion of the Divine Feminine. But in the circles of the Mystics the Holy Spirit was regarded as feminine, the Spouse of Divinity, and in the Wisdom-literature Wisdom herself.

As in the other great traditions, so also in pre-Christian Jewish Gnostic circles, the natural Trinity was a fundamental of their symbolism, and so also in many a system of the Christianized Gnosis.

The origin of the Dual Sonship, however, must in one direction at any rate, be sought for along that very obscure line of descent that is called Ophite (Naassene), and which has its roots in the pre-Christian Gnosis and the widespread Myth of Man (see H. i. 139-198).

THE DUAL SONSHIP.

A faint trace of this is preserved for us in a system which the polemical Refutation (I. xxx) of Irenæus associates with the Ophite tradition, but which Theodoret (Hær. Fab. I. xiv.) ascribes to the Sethians. Unfortunately the original Greek text of Irenæus is here lost, and we have to be content with the barbarous Old-Latin translation; in addition the Church Father is very hostile and contemptuous, and at no great pains to understand the objects of his detestation. Such as it is, however, we will set it down:

"But others again give forth portentous utterances: that there dwells in the Power of the Depth a certain Primal Light, blessed, indestructible, boundless; this is the Father of all and is called the First Man.

"They declare further that His Thought proceeding from Him, is the Son of Him who sends forth [His Thought]; and that this Thought is Son of Man, the Second Man.

"That below these again is the Holy Spirit; and below this Highest Spirit, the [Primal] Elements were separated forth--Water, Darkness, Abyss, Chaos; and on these was borne the Spirit, whom they call the First Woman.

"Subsequently, they assert, the First Man together with His Son, delighting in the Beauty of the Spirit, that is the Woman, and filling Her with Light, begat from Her Incorruptible Light, the Third Man, whom they call the Christ, Son of the First and the Second Man and of the Holy Spirit, the First Woman."

Here we have clearly set forth the idea of the Dual Sonship--though from a different point of view from that of our Poem--and of Man, Son of Man, a term that occurs frequently in the Gospels, and which so far scholarship refuses to explain gnostically, preferring to lose itself in the philological labyrinth of a quite unsatisfactory Aramaic Bar-N~ sh~ .

That the ruling idea of the Dual Sonship was widespread in Gnostic circles, both non-Christian and Christianized, may be seen from the following parallels, though where we are to seek the prototype of it--whether along some single line of Babylonian, Chaldæan, Magian, Syrian or Egyptian mystagogy, or as a common possession of Chaldæa and Egypt--is hard to say.

1. In the Mago-Chaldæan system underlying the early Simonian document The Great Announcement (see The Gnostic Crucifixion, pp. 40 ff.):

The Power of the Depth =	The Great Power, Incomprehensible Silence.
The First Man =	The Father, Mind of the Universals.
Man Son of Man =	Great Thought.
The First Woman, Holy Spirit or Breath =	The Middle Distance, Incomprehensible Air.
The Christ =	He who has stood, stands, and will stand.

2. In the system underlying the Chaldæan Oracles, a Greek mystery-poem of the first century in which Mago-Chaldæan material is "philosophized":

The Power of the Depth	=	God-nurturing Silence.
The First Man	=	The Father, Mind, Fire.
Man Son of Man, The Second Man	=	Mind of Mind, The Second Mind.
The First Woman	=	The Great Mother.
The Christ	=	The Æon (as Monad, Atom, Light-spark, Symbol).

3. Again in the system underlying the oldest extant treatise of the Trismegistic literature, "The Pœmandres" or "Man-Shepherd" (H. ii. 3 ff.):

The Power of the Depth	=	The Silence before the Voice.
The First Man	=	All-Father Mind.
Man Son of Man	=	Formative Mind, The Second Mind.
The First Woman	=	Nature.
The Christ	=	Man, Brother of the Formative Mind.

There is thus little doubt that in Gnostic circles, both pre-Christian and Christian, there was a clear tradition of Two Sons, one who remained, and one who went forth; and the one who went forth or returned was the Christ. Our Poem is therefore a Song of the Christ-Mystery.

"Thy Brother, Our Second," or Next-in-rank, is the Supernal Man, Son of Man; and the Christ, because of His Descent, and His winning of the Pearl of Self-consciousness in manifestation, is exalted to equality with the Supernal Son, or even to still higher rank; yet are they both one.

THE ROBE OF GLORY.

It is to be noted that there are two Vestures: the Robe of Glory and the Purple Mantle.

Now in the canonical scriptures John xix. 24 (cf. Matth. xxvii. 35, Mk. xv. 24, Lk. xxiii. 24, all of which look back to Psalm xx. 18) reads:

"They parted my Garments among them;

"And for my Vesture they cast lots."

The fourth Gospel (xix. 23) distinguishes the "Garments" and the "Vesture," adding that the "Coat" (chitÇn) "was without seam, woven from the top throughout."

Now the chitÇn, or tunica, was an under-garment, and was generally worn under a woollen cloak, or mantle (chlamys, or toga) during the day.

The writer of the fourth Gospel was a Mystic, and doubtless meant to convey an under-meaning to those who had "ears to hear."

As the "Garments" were divided into four among the "four soldiers," can it be that he intended to convey the idea of a Cloak of the four elements, and a Vesture of the one element, or quintessence, the complement of the four? At any rate this would be in keeping with the mystery-teaching concerning the "perfect body" or "body of resurrection," as may be seen from the Mithriac Ritual.

Whether or not he had any such intentions, and whether or not he had further the same ground-ideas in mind as those set forth by the Gnostic poet in our beautiful Hymn, must be left to the opinion of the reader according to his knowledge or ignorance.

The difference between the under-garment and mantle may be seen in many a Mithriac monument; while in the Mithriac Ritual we read (p. 27):

"Thou shalt behold a God. . . in a White Tunic and a Scarlet Mantle."

And again (p. 32):

"Thou shalt see . . . a God . . . clad in a Robe of Brightness."

The "Scarlet Mantle" is an exact parallel with the "Purple Mantle" of our Poem.

The nature of the Divine Robe, or, Glory, as a Heavenly Dwelling, was understood by Paul when he writes (I. Cor. v. I ff.):

"For know that if our house on earth of the [fleshly] tabernacle be dissolved, we have a God-made Building, a House not made with hands, eternal [lit. æonian] in the Heavens.

"For, indeed, we are groaning in this [habitation on earth], longing to be clothed with our Heaven-made Habitation."

Paul was well versed in Gnostic nomenclature; and the extended meaning of the Robe of Glory, as it was understood by the Mystics, may be grasped by the present-day Mystic who reads the following passages from one of the inspired outbursts of the beautiful Untitled

Apocalypse of the Coptic Gnostic Codex Brucianus:

"In this City it is that they move and live; it is the House of the Father, and the Vesture of the Son, and the Power of the Mother, and the Image of the Fulness [Pl' rÇ ma]." (F. p. 547).

And again:

"And they praised the One and Only One, and Conception [or Thought, the Mother], and the Mind-born Logos, praising the Three who are One, for through Him they became supersubstantial.

"And the Father took their whole Likeness and made it into a City or into a Man. He limned the Universe in His [sci. the Man's] Likeness--that is all these Powers.

"Each one of them knew Him in this City; all began to sing myriads of songs of praise to the Man or the City of the Father of the universe.

"And the Father hath taken His Glory and made it into a Vesture without for the Man. . . . He created His Body in the type of the Holy Pl' rÇ ma." (F. p. 566).

And yet again the Ineffable Vesture is sung of as follows:

"The First Monad hath sent Him an Ineffable Vesture, which is all Light and all Life, and all Resurrection, and all Love, and all Hope, and all Faith, and all Wisdom, and all Gnosis, and all Truth, and all Peace. . . .

"And in it is the universe, and the universe hath found itself in it, and knows itself therein.

"And it [sci. the Vesture] gave them all light in its Ineffable Light; myriads of myriads of powers were given it, in order that it should raise up the universe once for all.

"It gathered its vestures to itself, and made them after the fashion of a Veil which surrounds it on all sides, and poured itself over them, and raised up all, and separated them all according to order and law and forethought." (F. p. 557).

And yet once more from the same high document of deep mystic lore:

"He is the Man begotten of Mind, to whom Reflection gave form.

"Thou hast given all things to the Man. He weareth them like these garments, and putteth them on like these vestures, and wrappeth Himself with creation as with a mantle." (F. p. 562)

If we were to set down all the passages in Gnostic and allied literature connected with the mystery of the Robe of Glory, the Wedding Garment, and the rest of the Light-Vestures of the Soul, we should speedily exhaust the space of this little volume and of several other volumes.

We must, however, find room for a brief notice of the magnificent description of the Descent of the Vesture of Light on the Master, the Gnostic Transfiguration, in the Pistis Sophia (P.S. 5 ff.; F. pp. 259 ff.). The whole subject is treated more fully in my essay on "The Soul-Vestures," in The World-Mystery (2nd ed., pp. 117 ff.):

"But the Disciples saw not Jesus because of the Great Light in which He was, or which shone on Him; for their eyes were darkened because of the Great Light in which He was. They saw the Light only, sending forth a host of light-rays.

"And the light-rays were not like to one another. The Light was of various kinds, and it was of various types, from below above, each ray being more admirable than its fellow . . . in a Great Glory of immeasurable Light; it stretched from below the Earth right up unto Heaven. . . .

"It was of three degrees. The first was more admirable than the rest [? of the rays]; the second, which was in the midst, was more admirable than the first which was below it; and the third, which was above them all, was more admirable than the two below it."

The Master explains this mystery to His Disciples as follows:

"Lo, I have not put on my Vesture, and all authority hath been given me by the First Mystery. . . .

"It came to pass, when the Sun had risen in the East, that a Great Light-power descended, in which was my Vesture, which I had left behind in the Four-and-twentieth Mystery. . . .

"And I found a Mystery in my Vesture, written in Five Words of those from the Height . . . of which the interpretation is this:

"O Mystery that is Without, in the World, because of which All hath come into existence! This is the whole Out-going and the whole Up-going, which hath emanated all Emanations and all that is therein, because of which all Mysteries exist and all their Regions.

"Come unto us! For we are Thy Fellow-Members [or Limbs]; we are all one with Thee; we are one and the same. Thou art the First Mystery which hath existed from the beginning in the Ineffable before it came forth, and the Name thereof is all of us.

"Now, therefore, we all together draw nigh unto Thee at the Last Limit (that is, at the Last Mystery from Within); it is itself a portion of us.

"Now, therefore, we have sent Thee Thy Vesture, which indeed hath belonged to Thee from the beginning, which Thou didst leave behind in the Last Limit, which is the Last Mystery from Within, until its time should be fulfilled, according to the Command of the First Mystery.

"Lo, its time is fulfilled; clothe Thyself therewith!

"Come unto us! For we all draw nigh unto Thee to clothe Thee with the First Mystery and all His Glory, by Commandment of the same; in that the First Mystery hath given us it, consisting of two Vestures, besides the one that we have sent Thee, for Thou art worthy of them; for in sooth Thou art prior to us and came into being before us. Wherefore now hath the First Mystery sent Thee through us the Mystery of all His Glory, two Vestures."

The text then goes on to enumerate the Hierarchies of Æons, Powers, and Gods, which compose these Heavenly Garments—corresponding detail for detail with the whole emanative potencies of the Universe whereby the Garment of Deity is woven, and then continues its magnificent exposition; the Living Powers which form the Vesture speaking as follows on the Great Day "Be with us"--the moment of Supreme Perfection:

"Lo, therefore, have we sent Thee Thy Vesture, which no one from the First Law [or Precept] downwards hath known; for the Glory of its Light was hidden in it [sci. the Law], and all Regions from the First Law downwards have not known it.

"Make haste, therefore, clothe Thyself with this Vesture, and come unto us! For we draw nigh unto Thee, in order to clothe Thee with thy Two Vestures, which have been for Thee from the beginning with the First Mystery, until the time appointed by the Ineffable should be fulfilled.

"Come, therefore, to us quickly, that we may clothe Thee with them, until Thou hast fulfilled the whole Ministry of the Perfection of the First Mystery, the Ministry appointed by the Ineffable!

"Come, therefore, to us quickly that we may clothe Thee with them according to the Commandment of the First Mystery! For yet a little while, a very little while, and Thou shalt come to us and leave the world.

"Come, therefore, quickly, that Thou mayest receive Thy whole Glory, the Glory of the First Mystery!"

This gives us all the light we need to throw on the inner meaning of our Poem; it is the inner tradition intended for the initiated, whereas our Poem was intended to be circulated among the people. Which was prior? If the former, then we have found a terminus for the dating, if not of the Pistis Sophia as a whole, then of one of its "sources," and the date must be pushed back into the second century.

A STORY OF THE INFANCY.

But before we leave the Pistis Sophia there is another instructive passage that is reminiscent of the same ideas which underlie the words: "Unto me I took it and kissed it" (50); and also: "That we were twain in distinction, And yet again one in one likeness" (78). It is an otherwise unknown Story of the Infancy and runs as follows (P.S. pp. 120 ff.):

"And Mary [the Mother] answered and said:

"My Master, concerning the word which Thy Power prophesied through David, to wit: 'Grace and Truth met together, Righteousness and Peace kissed each other; Truth sprouted out of the Earth, and Righteousness looked down from Heaven'--Thy Power prophesied this word of old concerning Thee.

"When Thou wert a child, before the Spirit had descended upon Thee, whilst thou wert in vineyard with Joseph, the Spirit came from the Height, and came to me in my house, like unto Thee; and I knew Him not, and thought that He was Thou.

"And the Spirit said unto me: Where is Jesus my Brother, that I may go to meet Him?

"And when He had said this unto me, I was in perplexity and thought it was a phantom [come] to tempt me.

"So I took Him and bound Him to the foot of the bed that was in my house, until I had gone unto you--to Thee and Joseph, in the field--and found you in the vineyard--Joseph propping up the vines.

"It came to pass, therefore, when Thou didst hear me speaking the word unto Joseph, that Thou didst understand the word, and wert joyful and saidest: Where is He that I may see Him? Otherwise I await Him in this place.

"It came to pass when Joseph heard Thee saying these words, that he was troubled, and we went together, we entered the house, and found the Spirit bound to the bed. And we gazed on Thee and Him, and found Thee like unto Him.

"And He that was bound to the bed was loosed; He embraced Thee and kissed Thee, and Thou also didst kiss Him; and ye become one."

I am somewhat persuaded that under the apparently naïve details of this infancy story there is a concealed meaning. Once I gave a lecture in which I endeavoured to suggest what the nature of its under-meaning may have been, but it is too long to set down here.

It is apparently from another "source" of the P. S. document, and not due to the compiler.

THE TWO COURIERS.

The Two Couriers also pertain to the mystery hidden under the symbolism of the Twins which meets us everywhere in the ancient myths and legends of initiation; in reversed reflection they would be the Two Thieves crucified with Him.

In the Transfiguration-scene in the canonical Gospels, when the Master is clothed with Light, the Two are taken by the unknowing Disciples for Moses and Elias.

In The Gospel of Peter, in the story of the Mystery of the Resurrection, they are seen as Two Men, of the appearance of Light, whose heads reach unto heaven.

This mystic tradition may be compared with the more prosaic "two men in shining garments" of the third Gospel; while its Gnostic analogue may be seen in the Two Great Beings reaching unto heaven, of whom the precise mystic dimensions are given, in the Nazoræan, or Galilean, scripture, The Book of Elxai, that is The Book of the Hidden Power (see Did Jesus live 100 B.C.? pp. 365 ff.).

In the Pistis Sophia, as Receivers of Light, they are called Gabriel and Michael, who led "the Light-stream over Pistis Sophia"--the repentant faithful soul (P.S. 130 ff.), and who elsewhere in the same document take back the souls to the Light. They lead "the Light-stream into Chaos and bring it forth again" (P.S. 133).

In the Book of Enoch (lxxi. 3) it is Michael who brings Enoch before the most High, and Abraham to the Throne of God.

The Two Angels of opposite sex--allegorizing or substantializing the man's good and evil deeds--who lead the soul through the Middle Distance are native to the Magian and presumably Old Iranian traditions.

In Hellenic mythology and Hellenistic mystagogy it is Hermes who is the psychagogue and psychopomp, and he bears in his hand a Rod twined about with the Serpent Twins.

THE ALLEGORICAL GEOGRAPHY.

The geography of the way down from Hyrcania to Egypt, and back again, is consistent with itself (18-20, 69-71), but puzzling in some of its details.

Hyrcania was the mountainous region on the southern shores of the Caspian Sea.

The territory of Maish~ n lay between Mesopotamia and the sea; Maish~ n the city (For~ t Maish~ n = ? Messene) was in all probability the chief emporium of the sea-borne commerce of Babylonia and the West with India, and lay slightly to the south of the present-day Basra.

Babylonia was the Tigris-Euphrates valley.

Sarbā g is a puzzle. The best solution seems to be that it stands for the City of Babylon itself. Now, strangely enough, the Greek, in both traditions, renders Sarbā g by the "Labyrinth." This may possibly refer to the labyrinth of the streets of the great city. But it may also preserve for us a hint of how the geography was allegorized by the Gnostic exegetes; for "The Labyrinth" was a technical term of the Gnosis, as may be seen from a fine Naassene Hymn, two lines of which, referring to the soul, run as follows:

> "Now is born, with no way out for her; in misery
>
> She enters in her wandering the Labyrinth of ills." (H. i. 191).

Whatever the precise situation of the otherwise unknown Sarbā g may have been, it must be very patent to the Mystic that the Gnostic poet intended it for a certain stage of the descent of the soul, or spiritual mind, into the regions of manifestation.

Hoffmann (pp. 289 ff.) has attempted an interpretation on these lines. The Way of the Soul, he says, leads from (1) Heaven as the God-realm, through (2) the Firmament, to (3) the Earth--corresponding with the three natures of man: spirit, soul, and body.

He further sets forth a diagrammatic representation as follows:

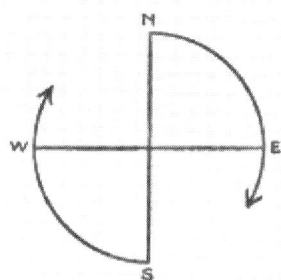

N = The Region of the Ineffable, the Mountain of the Gods, Hyrcania. This is the Over-world or Pleroma.

E = The Heaven of the Fixed Stars, Æther, the Midst, the Virgin of Light (of P.S.).

Between this and the Earth comes the Boundary of the Over-world and the World (=S), or Maishān.

Next comes the Earth-heaven or Firmament, Babel.

W = Egypt, the Earth and the Under-world.

 This seems to me a somewhat too elaborate scheme; but if it can stand, it strengthens the case for priority of the scheme underlying the Pistis Sophia to our Poem.

Maish~ n is the Mart of the Merchants of the East, and therefore should represent the borders or limit of the material world, or hylic cosmos, its uttermost region upwards.

Babel-land and Sarbāg would thus stand for the state or states lying between the region of direct commerce with the East (or Light-world)--that is, the region of the Heaven-world or Elysium--and the Earth-state.

These are presumably the states of the Middle Distance--that is, Hades; for in l. 50 we are told that the Letter is sealed:

"'Gainst the Children of Babel, the wicked, The tyrannical Daimons of Sarbāg."

These are presumably under the rule of the Prince of the Powers of the (Lower) Air.

The rest of our space may now be devoted to a few notes of detail, and to an endeavour to suggest some considerations of a mystical nature that may be of interest to those who delight in such studies, on the ground that the whole Poem is concerned with the mystery of the Light-spark, or Spiritual Man, or Son-ship, or Christ-nature.

NOTES.

The opening words seem to suggest, from the human point of view, the Birth of the Christ-nature and its state before it descends into manifestation, or drops into personality.

The "little child" may be taken to denote the Light-spark (or Ātmic ray), as it was symbolically termed by the Gnostics; in itself it is no "spark," but the potentiality of the Fullness (Plērōma) itself. To aid our dim intuition it may be regarded as "born" onto the plane of the spirit from the ever-divine states of the Fatherhood and Motherhood, of Divine Light and Life.

"Little child," or "little one," means also a certain stage of initiation, when the man below, the personal man, is bringing to birth, that is to consciousness, the spiritual or Christ nature in himself.

It is characterized by purity, innocence (harmlessness), spiritual instinct (not mind in its ratiocinative mode), childlikeness. In our Poem, however, it is not the man who is speaking, but the Spark or Son-ship.

The "Father's Kingdom" is the state of Ātman, and the "House" is spiritual Personality or Individuality, the Home of the Higher Self.

It is a state of Bliss, the activities of the Child are of the nature of Bliss; and the "Upbringers," or Nurturers, are the Arms of the Divine Life in which the Child is cradled. "Wealth" and "Glories" are characteristics of the Kingdom. The Nurturers, as Nurses of the Divine Infant, might be perhaps more appropriately characterized by "fulness" and "richness."

"From the East." "East" often does not so much refer to a particular state or a definite plane; it indicates rather a direction, which connotes as it were the power of cutting directly through planes. Birth from the East is not so much a birth viâ planes, that is a stirring of matter, as an inner way of immediate arrival. But in the text it does not seem to be used in such a precise sense.

The "Treasure" seems to denote the Jewels, that is, the senses or instincts, of the Spiritual Mind. There was a certain "binding up" of it; this suggests the first defining of space or limitation of the Spirit.

It was "large" and "light," spacious but as yet not heavy or possessed of gravity, that is tension or relation to personal environment.

The Treasure was carried in the "heart" of the man; that is, in the innermost substance of his nature.

"Land of Gilan". The Geli were a people who inhabited the district now called Gilan, on the south-west shore of the Caspian. Bevan, however, prefers "land of the upper ones," and the Greek has it also.

Ganzak, or Gazzak, was a district in Atropatene dharbaijan).

The Greek has: "Gold of the great treasures uncoined." Kā shā n is perhaps Kā shā n in Persia, north of Ispahan.

It may be that a precise symbolism, connected with the nature of the perfected "formal mind," may be hidden under the names of the precious stones, some of which are of uncertain translation. They would thus suggest a pure vesture of a formal nature, corresponding with the mineral kingdom, with which the soul or self is equipped or furnished.

The Greek glosses the Robe as "of gold tissue with jewels incrusted."

It is of "Gold" and "Silver"; that is, has "Sun" and "Moon" powers.

"Chalcedonies," or "Agates," are a puzzle; but the "iris-hued," or iridescent, colouring well represents the shimmer of all colours of the pure "glory," or purified "aura."

The Greek has "pearls" for "iris-hued [stones]."

All this is "bound" to the spiritual man by the power of the hardest of all the precious stones.

He is "armed" with it, according to the Greek. Compare "Armour of Sounding Light" of The Chaldæan Oracles, ii. 45.

Whether or not there is in the term "Adamant" (Diamond) a play on the Adamus (Adam, the Primal Man) of the Mysteries, must be left to the decision of the reader. It is of interest, however, in this connection to set down a passage from the Naassene Document. Referring to the allegorical "Rock" to which the souls cling in the Odyssey, the Jewish commentator writes:

"The 'Rock' means Adamas. This is: 'The Corner stone' which 'I insert in the Foundation of Zion.'

"By this [Foundation] he [Isaiah] means the plasm of man." (H. i. 161.)

"Purple Mantle." Purple is a sign of royalty; for our Poet is singing of a Royal Soul. (See The Chaldæan Oracles, ii. 74.)

Hoffmann makes the Mantle or Toga = anima naturaliter divina. Compare l. 26:

"And my rank did long for its nature."

"Stature" is in its root-sense a "standing upright," and may be compared with the idea of Him "who has stood, stands, and shall stand" of The Great Announcement. (See The Gnostic Crucifixion, p. 41.) It is the Spiritual Mind of man, his inner steadfastness and stability, and his own measurement and monument.

The "Compact," or Covenant or Ordinance, may be compared with the words of one of the Hymns of the Sophia (P.S. 64):

"Thy Commandment [or Statute], (O Light,) hath brought me Below, and I am descended like a Power of Chaos; my Power hath grown cold in me."

It was written "in the heart" (cf. l. 55). This means, mystically, written in the spiritual "blood" of the man, in the life-substance of him, in the very atoms of his substance. It was not engraved on the mind, but written deep down in the heart, so that it should not be forgotten.

Memory is connected with past, present, and future; but this record could not be really wiped out even when time should be no more.

The "Pearl" is the Living Gnosis, or again the self-realization of the Logos in man, or again the "Kingdom of Heaven," or rather the "Kingship of the Heavens."

But why should these living ideas be symbolized by a "pearl"--a precious thing, yet the product of disease?

If we may be permitted to speculate on the further meaning of a physical fact not known to the ancient Gnostics, we might suggest that Living Gnosis cannot be gained without the help of the Opposing Powers, the mystical Adversary.

Gnosis from one point of view is the union of the spiritual and personal man. When the spiritual self would attain to Divine consummation, there must be a descent into the spheres of personality, where people and things live, so to speak, within "shells." The spiritual man has to "steal" from within the Great Shell, or from within the shell side of things, that most precious gem which is the product of self-will or "disease"--that is of the "Opposer."

This mystery may also be called a "pearl" because, on the substance side of things, the man in whom Gnosis is born, or who is born in Gnosis, is for ever after wrapped in a pearly Glory, or his substance becomes pearl-like to the opened eye of the seer.

The oyster, or "jelly fish" or plasm, is the "shell" of personality, is the man of "flesh," or unevolved buddhic substance. The Impersonal Spirit, or atman, at an earlier stage of evolution, descends and stirs this substance to create, broods over it, and it creates a "pearl," which from the personal and selfish point of view is not at first advantageous to the "jelly fish."

This "pearl" again, later on, is a pure substance or ichor which the buddhic nature creates or secretes when atman begins to energize in the man.

The "loud-breathing Serpent" is Typhon, the Opposer; the Lord of the passions or opposing forces of the planes of form.

The Greek has "the Serpent the Swallower," and Hoffmann has "poison-breathed."

The "Sea" is, of course, the Ocean of Genesis, the manifested planes, or states of manifestation; it is the Ocean of life-and-death, or repeated birth, the Ever-becoming, the Samsā ra of the Brā hmans and Buddhists. The "poison," if "poison-breathed" is the correct translation, reveals Typhon (Apeps); it is the cause of the "disease" operated by the Opposer.

The Pearl is thus again perfected root-form, or the "permanent atom" of experience, so to speak, to which the Robe of Glory and Mantle of Royalty can be attached, and so union be achieved between the upper and lower.

The Robe is the Cosmic Texture of Light and Life, and is stamped and sealed by the Great Name of the Spiritual Individuality.

"Thy Brother," as we have seen in the comments (p. 45), means from one point of view the Demiurgic or Architectural or

Building Power, in an inner mystical sense the Obedient Opposer of Life, own Twin to atman. In a still more mysterious sense that is not brought out in our Poem, atman, the Christ, may be said to go to seek His lost Brother (in the Christianized Gnosis this was generally His lost Sister or Spouse, the Sophia or Wisdom); they unite in the Mystery of the Sacred Marriage or At-one-ment, and become Heir of Infinity and Eternity.

The Christ descends and carries off or saves the Pearl, thus attaching Himself to the Pure Essence, purified by suffering, born of the energy of the Opposer within form, and so wins the way back to the Kingdom. The Opposer is Next-in-rank to God.

It has been suggested that because of this "twin" idea our Poem has been very appropriately inserted into the Acts of Judas Thomas, that is, of Judas the Twin of Jesus; and certainly this hidden mysticism of Judas the Twin and Judas the Betrayer was highly elaborated by the Gnostics, so that we even find traces of a Gospel of Judas.

The "Couriers," or Messengers (lit. Letter-carriers, Per. Parwã nk§ n), are, in one sense, a Twin-Ray from the Mind of the Master of all masterhood, Boundless Light, the true Father-Mother of the Soul that is striving to bring itself to birth.

The "Way" from the "East," in its more immediate mystical meaning, denotes a direct path through matter by means of a Ray of the True Sun, of the nature of a "lightning-flash," as set forth so graphically in the mystery-poem known as The Chaldæan Oracles (II. 19); it "blazes" directly through matter, and does not meander through the labyrinth of the planes. In our Poem, however, there is a descent through planes or states.

Maishã n perhaps connotes the plane of the Quintessence or One Element (Buddhi), the complement and source of the four.

The Land of Babel suggests presumably the confused sounds (the confusion of tongues) of the personal "astral" or emotional state; and the walls of Sarbã g may stand for the city of the personal formal mind, the labyrinth of personal-mind-made planes.

Thereon comes the plunge into the physical body (Egypt), when the direct guidance of the Twin-Ray ceases for a time.

In mystical physiology this Serpent may signify something within the "blood," or perhaps the "elemental essence," which must sleep, or be quieted, before the heavenly ichȫr can be born, or the "pearl," the real root-purity within form, be detached from the downward current, and attached again to atman. Compare A Mithriac Ritual (p. 28):

"For that a man--I, N.N., Son of N.N. (fem.)--born of the mortal womb--of N.N. (fem.)--and of spermatic ichȫr, yea of this ichȫr, which at Thy Hands to-day hath undergone the transmutation of re-birth [or birth from Above]--one, from so many tens of thousands, transformed to immortality in this same hour, by God's good pleasure, of God transcendent Good--,[a man, I say] presumes to worship Thee, and supplicates with whatsoever power a mortal hath."

Compare this with the ancient reading of the Great Utterance at the Mystical Baptism Rite:

"Thou art my Beloved Son; this day have I begotten thee!"

The "lodging" is, literally, a "lodging-place for travellers"--that is to say, an inn, or caravanserai. The Greek has simply "den" or "hole." And here we may call to mind the following paragraph from Hippolytus' summary of Valentinian doctrine:

"And this material man is, according to them, as it were, an inn, or dwelling-place, at one time of the soul alone, at another time of the soul and daimonian existences [elemental essences], at another of the soul and words [logoi, or angels or reasonable essences] which are words sown from Above--from the Common Fruit of the Plȫrȫma [the Christ] and Wisdom [the Divine Mother]--into this world, dwelling in the body of clay together with the soul, when daimons ceased to cohabit with her." (F. p. 352).

This is the body in Egypt, or the hylic world or cosmos of gross matter. As the original Jewish writer of the canonical Apocalypse tells us (Rev. xi. 7,8):

"'The Beast that ascendeth out of the Abyss shall make war with' them, 'and overcome them,' and slay them.

"And their carcase [shall lie] in the street of the Great City, which is spiritually called 'Sodom' and Egypt."

To which the Christian over-writer adds:

"Where also our Lord was crucified."

Who this noble youth from the East may be mystically, I am unable precisely to conjecture, unless it refers to the "voice of conscience," the spiritual tendencies in the natural man. The reader, however, may be reminded of the supposition in the Preamble (p. 13), that historically it may be autobiographical.

Preuschen interprets it in terms of the Gospel-story; the Son being the Christ, and the noble youth Jesus. But this does not work out.

I have adopted the reading of Nicetas; the Syriac "I warned him" seems hopelessly confusing.

Before the true reunion can take place, not only must the "evil one" be "saved," but the "saviour" must be "lost," and dealt with "treacherously"; the Christ must be "betrayed." Without this there would not be perfect balance. It is the formal mind that betrays.

The "food" is the "food of the world" of P.S. 346; compare also the passage (ibid. 282):

"And the Babe eateth of the Delights [or Food-stuffs] of the World of the Rulers; and the Power absorbeth from the portion of the Power which is in the Delights; and the Soul absorbeth from the portion of the Soul that is in the Delights; and the Counterfeit Spirit absorbeth from the portion of the Evil which is in the Delights and in its desires; whilst the Body absorbeth from the unperceptive Matter (Hyl') which is in the Delights."

With the forgetfulness, or oblivion, induced by the Victuals, or Delights, compare a passage from one of the Hymns of Repentance of the Sophia (P.S. 63):

"They have taken away my Light, and my Power is dried up.

"I have forgotten my Mystery which I performed from the beginning.

"Because of the din [or confusion] of the Fear and Power of Arrogant [the Opposer, the Serpent of self-interest], my Power hath failed me."

The "draught of oblivion," or forgetfulness, is also described at length in the Pistis Sophia (see, for instance, pp. 281, 385).

The "weight of their victuals" is paralleled in P.S. (281) by the "very heavy weight of forgetfulness."

In a wider and more mystical sense the food that atman now eats has to do with the formal mind in the mode of subject and object; thus is its simplicity differentiated, and it becomes food and food-eater, and so is brought down into time and objects; and then the curse of memory and forgetfulness begins, and the true natural instinctual awareness of the Spirit sleeps.

The spiritual germ has now become embedded in man and is fast asleep in substance; and a great impulse, an earthquake, is required to arouse it and awake it from the dead.

For "And this is the counsel they came to," Bevan gives: "So they wove a plan on my behalf."

If "plan" is the key-word, then, taking it in conjunction with the idea of the Letter to which every Prince, or Noble, set his Name, we may hazard the conjecture that, in one sense, it may be taken as referring to the mystery of re-incarnation; it suggests the weaving, out of all previous lives, some sort of a plan or destiny, stamped with the Name of every Prince.

The Princes may be thought of as "facets" of the King; they represent the "faces" or "personæ" of the Spiritual Mind, or Highest Self. They would thus stand for not all the prior existences of the man, but rather such lives as had been able to manifest some portion of that Spiritual Mind.

The Letter might thus be said to be woven out of the "substance" of previous lives, to which each proper person or facet of the spiritual Wholeness supplies its due share. This immediately attracts the soul in its last incarnation, for it is itself.

This Letter or Plan, woven out of the permanencies of a man's previous incarnations, is sealed by the Father of atman, so that it shall not be torn to pieces as it descends through the regions or planes. It would naturally have a tendency to be scattered; its substance would naturally remain on the plane of substance, its mind-tendencies on the plane of mind; but that would be to be no more permanencies from all the planes, the fruitage of experience.

These are now gathered together into one Plan which is sealed by the Father of universals, or wholenesses or monads or æons, and so it continues to be whole even until it reaches the man, "right down" on the physical plane or in his natural body; and that is how wholeness in consciousness is born. It is a sort of germ of wholeness.

"King of kings." Compare Rev. xix. 16:

"And He hath in His Vesture and on His Thigh a Name written: King of kings and Lord of lords."

"Remember thy glorious Robe," and "The Book of the Heroes." Compare Rev. iii. 5:

"He who thus conquereth [by not defiling his garments] shall be clothed in White Robes, and I will not blot his Name out of the Book of Life."

Every man has his "book" and there is a Great Book. See Rev. xx. 12:

"And I saw the Dead, the great and little, standing in the Presence of the Throne, and [their] 'books were opened' [Dan. vii., 10]. And another Book was opened, which is '[The Book] of Life' [Dan. xii., 1]."

The Eagle, or Hawk, was the name of the highest grade of the Mithriaca--the Fathers. See A Mithriac Ritual (p. 18), where the Father's prayer ends:

"So that I, Eagle as I am, by my own self may soar to Heaven, and contemplate all things."

The Eagle-letter--which may be paralleled with the Descent of the Dove in the Baptism-Mystery--flew in the air the Bright Æther of the Supernal Realms, or the state of Divine Breath (atman); as it contacted the inmost or spiritual plasm of the man, his Buddhic nature, or the nature of his Depth, the Depth of his substance, it became "all sound" or "all speech."

The Buddhic nature is the Quintessence or One Element, the Aith' r or Æther, the Shining One; just as in Sanskrit a-kā sha is par excellence the Very Shining One, and its root-characteristic is "sound."

It was a true Bath-Kol, or Voice from Heaven, as the mystical Rabbis called it. Lit. Bath-Kol = Daughter of the Voice; that is to say, Echo of the Word or Name.

This Voice is the Inner Voice, the Voice Within, the Voice of the Silence. The "sound of its winging," or "the sound of its rustling," suggest another great symbol: the rustling or the activities of the "leaves" (powers and permanencies) on the man's true "Tree of Life," as the Wind or Divine Breath stirs them, thus awaking them to true activity and life.

"I took it and kissed it," etc. Thereby the two united; the "seal" which held it together as a wholeness was "loosed," and there was union. The Plan and Heart united, atom matched atom in "Mind" and "Blood." The Intelligible married the Sensible, and the Christ was born, the Eternal Memory.

"E'en as it stood in my heart writ." It is written by the Scribe of the Gods, Thoth the Divine, the Tongue and Heart of the Eternal. Compare II. Cor. iii., 2:

"Ye are our Letter written in our hearts."

"Filthy and unclean garments"--that is, the man's unrhythmic "bodies" or rather "vehicles." He leaves his personal-plane garments or vehicles behind on each plane, like a butterfly leaving his grub-case; only these do not die, or go into trance, they go on with their "filthy" or "daily" duties. They are the bodies of "dross." (See The Chaldæan Oracles, ii. 38).

His Great Plan, or Spiritual Mind-and-Substance, goes on before, precedes and proceeds. Its Voice or Life is its feminine power that awakens and brings to birth; its Light is its masculine potency that guides, controls, orders--the mode that happens after the awakening or resurrection.

The "fabric of silk" and "letters of red" suggest Buddhic substance and atmic radiance.

Burkitt translates:

"For it began to make its silken folds to glow."

And so the "Spark" passes "up" or "in" through the planes, though indeed it does not move; the Spark becomes a Flame. It is the life and journey of a Spark and not of any man-neophyte; though of course the life and journey of any initiate would have many things in common.

"The meeting-place of the merchants." This and the next line seem to be a doublet.

Father-Mother, the Supreme Mystery, give the Glory-Robe of Spiritual Life and Light to the Twin-Powers of Spiritual Mind, to bestow it on the returning Victor (or Prodigal) ascending the Sacred Way in Triumph.

The Robe is sent down from Hyrcania, which for the Parthians was the Mount of the Gods, the Height of Heaven, their Meru.

"The Glory looked like my own self."

This is the same idea as that which underlies the mirror-play of Iacchos, the Young Bacchus of the Mysteries. Compare also II. Cor. iii. 18:

"With unveiled face mirroring the Glory of the Lord, we are transformed into the same Likeness [or Image] from Glory to Glory as by the Breath of the Lord."

Burkitt translates:

"Myself I saw as in a glass before my face."

When the illuminated neophyte first sees the Self in all things, he sees it as himself reflected in all things. This is a great danger for many.

"The King of Kings' Image" suggests that originally the Embroidered Robe had been woven by the Mother only; but now it is stamped all over with the Image or Likeness of the Father.

"With Sapphires." Compare Ezekiel i. 26:

"And above the Firmament that was over their heads was the likeness of a Throne as the appearance of a sapphire stone: and upon the likeness of the Throne was the likeness as the appearance of a Man upon it."

And also Exodus xxiv. 10:

"And they saw the God of Israel: and there was under His Feet as it were a paved work of sapphire stone, as it were the Body of Heaven in his clearness."

"The Motions of Gnosis." There is a suggestion here of a certain dramatic state of consciousness where, by the man's own activities, he talks to himself.

The Robe is as it were the one uniting substance, or quintessence, which holds all things in its embrace, and with it comes the idea of reflection from oneself onto it; so that when the illumined seer contemplates it all the activities or motions of any object become knowledges, or everything seems to stir as if to speak, or become vocal, so that by these activities vital knowledge or gnosis is increased. It is the self talking to the self by means of action.

I follow Burkitt's emended version in his review of Preuschen.

"The Glory of Him who had sent it." Compare Rev. xxi. 23:

"For the Glory of God did lighten it [the Heavenly City], and the Lamb is the Lamp thereof."

The Greek "sweet-sounding" is rendered by Hoffmann as "water-organs," and he refers to Rev. i. 15:

"And His Voice as the sound of many waters."

And also Rev. xix. 6:

"And I heard as it were the Voice of a great multitude, and as the Voice of many waters, and as the Voice of mighty thunderings, saying, Alleluia!"

And again Jeremiah li. 16, 55:

"When He uttereth His Voice there is a multitude of waters."

"Because the Lord hath spoiled Babylon, and destroyed out of her the Great Voice; when her waves do roar like great waters, a noise of their voice is uttered."

Professor Burkitt writes:

"The remains of yet another stanza of the Hymn appear in Syriac. Only three lines are preserved; one is untranslatable, the second is utterly unmetrical, and the third--which appears to be the concluding line of the Poem--contains a very doubtful word. Probably the copy used by the editor who inserted the Hymn in The Acts of Thomas was badly damaged at the end. The fragments, thus completed, seem to be genuine, for we almost require some mention of the Pearl at the end of the Poem. I cannot attempt to venture the two missing lines, but the general sense appears to be as follows:"

Now, while with acclamation all His courts resound,

I wait until His gracious Promise be fulfilled:

That with Him to the Royal Council I should go,

And with my Pearl appear before them at His side.

Whatever may be its precise interpretation--and the Mystic at any rate knows that in vital things there cannot possibly be one formal interpretation only--there will be few who will not admit that this ancient Poem of the Gnosis is beautiful. For ourselves, we end with the hope that, when it is better known, no few may find it inspiring and illuminating also.

Note.--Journal of Theological Studies (London, April, 1908), vol. ix. No. 35, p. 473, in a review by C. H. W. Johns of Emil Behren's Assyrisch-babylonische Briefe Kultischen Inhalts aus Sargonidenzeit (Leipzig, 1906):

"The mention of Nabā's writing the 'Credit on account' of the King and his sons in the 'Book of life to last for ever' is noteworthy. Deeply interesting are the pilgrimages of the King's 'double' and the royal cloak (or pallium?)."

Printed in Great Britain
by Amazon